Raised Bed Gardening

Growing Vegetables for Beginners (B&W Version)

By

KENDRA K.

Table of Contents

Introduction

There is nothing like looking over a well-tended garden filled with row upon row of beautiful shades of green foliage, colorful blooms or lush, healthy vegetables. However, it can take years of hard work, toiling away to achieve this picture I just painted. While some gardeners love spending hours in their gardens, mixing soil, tilling it, watering and weeding, not everyone has that much time on their hands or the inclination to spend so much of their free time on gardening.

It is, however, quite possible to have a vegetable garden with plentiful crops without having to spend too many hours tending it. Even if you have limited space, you can still end up with a variety of tasty vegetables for your table.

The answer is a raised bed vegetable garden. Not only do raised beds make vegetable gardening less of a chore, it is also a lot easier. You can grow more plants in raised beds than in the same sized area on the ground. The beds are higher so no more backbreaking work or kneeling down between rows to do the weeding or harvesting. Raised beds are very convenient; if you spread mulch along the paths between your beds, you can quickly run out while you are cooking to cut a handful of herbs without getting your shoes muddy or dirty.

Raised beds are attractive landscape features. They make your garden look neat and tidy and you can even dress them up with details like corner posts or paint them to match the color of your garden furniture.

Now I will proceed to explain how to go about making your own raised bed garden, how to tend your plants, which vegetables to select and finally I will provide you with some useful tips to make sure you will enjoy an abundant harvest of all your favorite veggies right through the season.

Chapter 1

Why Raised Bed Vegetable Gardening

Traditional gardeners have been making use of raised beds to grow their vegetables for many years. They would double dig the beds, creating circular or rectangular mounds a foot or so high with the sloping edges on the sides of the beds. This is especially effective in areas that receive lots of rain since it guarantees good drainage. Additionally, it allows a bit more space to grow your veggies.

Companion planting works perfectly on raised beds. Those vegetables which need more space for their roots like carrots would be planted on top while others like leeks and onions would fill up the space on the sides of your beds. The latter repel pests and would act as a shield for the carrot plants on the top of the bed.

These are but a few of the numerous benefits of gardening in raised beds. Therefore, it is not surprising to find that our modern-day gardeners are turning their attention with more frequency to this method. They have added a twist though, now solid frames replace these sloping sides to give the raised beds a distinct and well-defined structure. What this means is that you can make the beds as high or tall as you want them to be without the danger of soil runoff when it rains.

It might sound like a huge job, but these modern raised gardening beds are easy to assemble or build by yourself. Frames can be built with concrete blocks, timber or bricks and then filled with many organic materials mixed with soil. You will find kits ready for assembling as well as prefabricated plastic containers at almost any gardening center. Now anyone and everyone can easily and successfully grow their vegetables in raised beds.

I will now point out some of the many benefits of this gardening method.

1.   Excellent Aeration

The older, traditional way to create raised beds is simply to dig up the soil, piling it into rows. You can follow this method and then support the two sides by using solid frames. Otherwise, place your frames in place and then fill them up with compost, farmyard manure mixed with quality soil. Whichever way you choose to do it, your plants will flourish in this enriched soil and its loose structure will allow excellent air circulation around all the roots.

We know that the different parts of plants all need to breathe, and so do the roots. For example during photosynthesis, the leaves take in carbon dioxide and expel oxygen. If your plant sits in compact soil, the roots will suffocate and will not succeed in developing fully. This is because they need good aeration for their roots to be able to absorb the essential nutrients in the soil. To explain further; the soil bacteria convert the nitrogen in the little air pockets into nitrate salts and nitrate, thus providing the macronutrients for the plant. Without sufficient air, there is a lack of nitrogen and therefore less nutrients will be available to the plant.

It is clear that the population of microbes in your vegetable soil must be kept healthy and this is made possible with good aerated soil. The balance of anaerobic and aerobic bacteria should be maintained as they all play their different roles to enhance the fertility of the soil.

2.   Good Drainage

Even during a downpour of rain, your raised beds will render good drainage. No wonder this method is so popular in the tropics with its heavy rainfall. Because the soil has such a loose texture, water will seep slowly into the bed instead of a making a quick runoff with the accompanying washing away of all fertile topsoil. Furthermore, all the excess water can easily drain away.

Although most plants do not mind moisture at all, they hate to get their feet wet. Firstly, all that water around their roots will make breathing almost impossible. Secondly, too much moisture will promote fungal and bacterial diseases. Lastly, excess water drenching the soil can change its pH level and raise the acidity. Plants which prefer more neutral or slightly alkaline soil will suffer as a result.

Some plants, for example those that live in bogs are adapted to grow in drenched soil but most plants prefer soil with a twenty five percent-moisture level. Raised beds will not allow water stagnation while at the same time keep your soil quite evenly moist because the water is soaked into the lowest levels of your beds quickly.

3.   The Spreading of Roots

Although plant roots can be quite persistent in their effort to grow, they will find it difficult to do so in tightly compacted soil. In loose soil they can grow and spread out to their hearts' contend. Furthermore, a framed bed will retain the moisture after watering a lot longer than the more traditionally raised beds because the frames prevent water loss on the sides of the beds more effectively. Drying out of the beds can therefore be prevented and good root spreading will follow.

Plants growing in non-raised garden beds generally have a very shallow system of roots since they find it impossible to penetrate through the more compact soil deeper down, unless of course you go to the trouble of tilling the soil deeply before you plant your vegetables. This means that the plant roots are unable to get to the moisture kept in the deeper layers, which in turn may lead to dehydration of the plant when the moisture on the surface evaporates. Well-developed root systems anchor your plants. It also enlarges the potential food source area from which the plant can gather its nutrients and water. Vegetable plants in particular, need enough of both to encourage vigorous growth and maximum yield during their relatively short growing season.

4.   Minimum Risk of Compact Soil

A raised bed will not completely deter your smaller pets like dogs and cats from digging and rolling around in your gardening soil, but it definitely will keep humans and larger pets or animals at bay. This will prevent the tamping down of the soil. The ideal width for your raised beds is three to four feet, making it easy for you to do your gardening chores such as weeding, harvesting and fertilizing without having to step onto the beds.

The floods which sometimes occur after a heavy downpour can also compact the soil of cultivated fields. Wet soil is heavy and will sink down and fill all the little air pockets. Once the water has evaporated, you will be left with a dense, hard layer that is not very accommodating for the plants. Raised beds allow the water to drain away much quicker, preventing floods to cause soil compaction.

5.   Improved Weed Control

Sick and tired of weeding? A raised bed garden is the answer. In a normal vegetable plot, you will find it hard to get rid of all the frustrating weeds no matter how dedicated you are. They just seem to take over all the time.

When you cultivate the soil for normal vegetable beds, you expose lot of the weed seeds that have been lying dormant underground shielded from the sun. The exposure to sunlight and extra moisture they receive during irrigation will provide them with the opportunity to start sprouting, just what they have been waiting for. Very quickly, they will feed on the nutrient-rich soil prepared for your vegetable plants and begin to flourish.

You can make use of the option to fill your raised beds with relatively weed-free soil and compost. If a few stray weeds appear, your raised beds with its loose soil will make weeding a breeze. A good tip is to fill up your raised beds with as many plants as will grow in it so that they will suffocate and outgrow any stubborn weeds that may try their luck.

6. Easier than Amending Existing Soil

Garden soil greatly varies from area to area; sometimes it is more alkaline and chalky, often it is too acidic and plants will not thrive without your intervention. Vegetables in general like slightly acidic to neutral soil, anything with a pH level of between 5.5 and 7.5. Having said that, there are exceptions. Blueberries and tomatoes, for instance, like more acidic soil while asparagus and broccoli prefer to have their roots in sweeter soil.

The remedy for alkaline soil is to add Sulphur, for acidic soil lime can be added. Sometimes applications have to be repeated a number of times to get the desired effect but a downpour can undo all your hard work in a flash. It is not a simple, straightforward process to change the intrinsic nature of any type of soil.

If you plan to cultivate different kinds of vegetables, raised beds will give you the option of which soil you choose. On top of that, you can now fill up different raised beds with the type of soil each variety of vegetable prefers. The addition of lots of compost, something most gardeners usually do, makes it easier to sustain the soil's neutrality.

7. Garden on Top of Existing Turf

You have made the decision to start your own vegetable garden, but the task of having to dig up and clean the existing turf presently growing on the area you have targeted is just too daunting. Do not despair; raised vegetable beds can be built straight on top of your grass without having to dig up any sods.

Mark your area, and then place multiple layers of cardboard and newspaper on the area. Erect your frames and then simply continue to fill them with grass clippings, soil, sand, decomposed farmyard manure and compost. Plant your seeds or seedlings in this rich mixture and you have started your garden without too much backbreaking labor.

8. Avoid Root Run from Larger Plants and Trees

Sometimes you will find that the only available space left in your garden for your vegetables is near a number of well-established trees. These trees have massively huge roots to anchor them to the ground and will devour all the nutrients in the soil, leaving very little for your vegetable plants. You may be able to get rid of some of these invasive roots, but it is an impossible task to get completely rid of them all. Using chemicals to try to kill the roots is not an option because these very same chemicals can harm or even kill your vegetable plants. However, your raised beds will be safe from this problem since tree roots generally grow downwards and will not reach into the raised beds.

9. More Effective Pest Control

Creepy crawlies are true to their description, they usually enter vegetable patches this way, crawling away until they find food. Encountering an obstacle like a solid frame will definitely deter some of them from crawling up. They may just pick the easier option of continuing along the ground. To protect your plants from soil parasites like nematodes, line your raised beds along the sides and the bottom with plastic. If you fear annoying rodents burrowing their way into your beds, use a netting of wire, placing it at the bases of your beds.

Overall, it will be easier to rid your beds of the various offenders just because they are more accessible. Applying chemical or natural pesticides or picking out invaders by hand is a lot less cumbersome if you do not have to bend down to ground level all the time. Everything, including nasty pests will be more visible to the eye too. Walking along your raised beds, inspecting your plants regularly you can quickly detect infestations and deal with them immediately. Remember; the sooner you tackle any pests the easier it will be to rid your vegetable garden of them.

10.   Extra Available Space

Raised beds in the traditional fashion provide more space for plants growing along the sides of the beds. Although this advantage is not applicable to framed beds, they can provide additional space in another manner. Many of the plants growing along the side edges of the frames will extend over these side edges, leaving more room for other plants on the top surface of the bed. More light will be able to reach the plants as well.

Those varieties of tomatoes that normally will need staking can simply be allowed to grow downwards instead of upwards. Make sure the beds you plant them in are high enough. Strawberries and the vines of sweet potatoes tumbling down the sides of your raised beds will make a very pretty picture in your garden and create a luxurious aspect.

11.   Extended Growing Season

We all know how long it takes the ground to thaw in spring but raised beds speed up this thawing process. This means that you can start transplanting your seedlings much earlier in the season, giving them a wonderful head start. If the area where you live has a short window period to grow your edibles in the outside garden, this extra time will make a huge difference.

Some vegetables, for instance onions, need a fairly long season to grow to maturity. Three to four months are needed for onions sets and if you grow them from the seeds, it will take even longer. Seeds give you a much larger choice as only a few varieties are generally available as sets. Making use of this advantage of choice means that you will need more time. Fortunately, onion seedlings like cooler weather, so plant them as soon as the soil in your raised beds has thawed.

Towards the end of the autumn, you can also extend your veggies' growing season; just place a few hoop covers onto your bed frames. This is easily done by installing pipe brackets made of metal from which you can attach or remove the hoop covers when necessary. Custom made covers in plastic or glass can be fitted for your individual raised beds as well.

12.   Intensive Gardening with Higher Yield

It is a fact that a higher yield will be obtained by growing your veggies in raised beds rather on flat ground beds. Attributing factors are the good aeration of the soil and extensive root run but the main cause is the intensive nature of this kind of gardening. Raised beds allow you to plant a greater variety of different kinds of vegetables closer together than could be done on flat ground.

Because the soil used in these raised beds contains more organic matter and compost, it is rich enough to support quite a number of extra plants, definitely more than usual. The plants will completely fill up the beds as they continue to grow with their foliage touching. The close proximity of the plants will prevent weeds from flourishing too.

13.   Solution for Mobility Challenged Gardeners

Not all gardeners are young, energetic, and healthy people. Many experienced gardeners find it difficult to continue bending down for weeding and tending their vegetable patches as they grow older and experience health challenges. Raised beds can be built or assembled to the exact width or height that will suit every individual. It can even be planned and laid out in a fashion to accommodate wheel chair users and allow them freedom of movement to plant and harvest their vegetables easily.

Even if you do not face any of these challenges, you will find it a relief to see to those vegetable plants that need constant attention if they are raised off the ground. Backbreaking work is never fun and may even cause injuries. Salad vegetables and herbs need frequent harvesting and popping out into the garden to pick a few herbs for your meal will be a lot easier if you do not have to bend down all the time.

14.   Portability

If you find that your vegetable plants are not exposed to enough sunlight in their current spot, you can just move your raised bed without too much effort. Portability is one of the advantages of this method of gardening. Beds with wire bottoms can simply be dragged to a brighter location. Otherwise, dismantle the frames and then reassemble your beds in their new spots. With care you can move the plants as well as the soil contend without any damage.

A very practical solution is to buy raised beds that are ready-made and fitted with casters. They are easily moved around and if early frost overtakes you, they can even be rolled into your heated garage to save your plants.

There are quite a number of variations on the theme of raised bed gardening like square foot, hay bale and keyhole gardening. They all assist in making growing your own food less of a challenge and a lot more rewarding, something the modern age gardener appreciates.

Chapter 2

Raised Beds: Site Preparation

One of the questions most frequently asked about raised beds for growing vegetables is just how tall they should be. There is no definite answer to this question, I am afraid. There is no 'ideal height'; it is completely up the individual. However, there are certain considerations that you must keep in mind. These include the soil conditions under the beds, the costs involved, the depth of the soil required for your specific crop and of course, which height would allow you to work comfortably in your raised beds. This last aspect should take priority if you are a matured gardener.

Preparation of the Ground

Double Dig

Although the plants in your raised beds will be provided with their own rich soil, some of them may grow roots that extend into the soil underneath the beds to search for additional nutrients and moisture. Therefore, it is important to prepare the soil below by double digging it. This must be done before you start on your raised beds and once done, need not be repeated.

Double digging simply means the depth to which you have to dig up the soil; it is approximately twenty-four inches deep, or in other words, two lengths of the blade of your shovel. Remove all the hard rocks and debris that could obstruct roots from growing down into the ground. Keep your eyes open for other large roots entering into this space. For instance, trees that grow nearby can send their roots to more than fifty feet diagonally underneath the surface searching for nutrients and water. Double digging will provide an extended reservoir of water and nutrients, which your plants' sturdier, deeper roots can have accessed to.

Digging up the ground also allows you to have a closer look at the status of the underlying soil, and to decide which amendments should be made. If it resembles clay, for instance, peat should be used to lighten it in order to aerate it and improve the drainage.

Improving the Subsoil

You have cleared the ground area of debris and rock and finished your double digging. If needed, you can now add some peat moss that will lighten your soil. Because peat has an acidic nature, you have to balance the pH level of the soil by adding lime. Sprinkle some rock phosphate over the plot and mix in with the soil. Your ground area is now ready for the raised plant bed, so assemble the frames and fill up with rich soil. When you almost reach the top of the raised bed, add compost and fertilizer. Do not add the compost and fertilizer too long before the season to avoid early, unexpected spring rainfalls to flush them too far down into your soil.

Ideal Height for Raised Beds

Consider Drainage

Raised beds have an aesthetic appeal, which speaks to many gardeners, but they also allow for proper drainage of the soil in which your veggies will be grown. In general, most raised beds are eleven inches tall, which is equal to that of two 2 by 6 standard boards. (In actual fact the measurements are 1.5 by 5.5 inches.) The reason why this height is most popular is that it provides adequate drainage for the majority of crops. The best results can be achieved if you allow for another twelve inches at least of rich soil underneath your raised bed. That will give your veggie plants up to twenty inches of good soil. Remember that raised beds usually end up not filled to the brim with soil; after every watering the soil will compress somewhat. You will need this extra space later to add some mulch.

Two factors contribute to the earlier warming up of the soil in raised beds during the spring: Firstly, the soil is always well above the ground level and the second aspect is the good drainage in these beds. Gardeners can therefore start transplanting much earlier and so lengthen the growing season of their veggies. To shield the young, vulnerable seedlings from a late frost or strong winds, place cold frames over the beds. Once the seedlings are stronger and better established, these frames can simply be removed and used elsewhere if needed.

Consider Bending Down

Young gardeners who are fit and energetic might not even waste time thinking about this aspect since going on your knees or bending down to attend to your plants is easy and you take it in your stride. People who suffer from backache or strain, or those whose mobility have been impaired will need higher raised beds to help lighten their gardening chores. Beds can be in a range of eight to twenty four inches high. You will quickly notice the huge difference between tending these various beds. Taller beds are just so much more comfortable when you have to set in transplants, till the soil, weed and harvest. It is not necessary to put extras strain on your back at all.

Cross Supports for Taller Beds

It is commonsense that taller beds will hold more volume so you have to keep this in mind when you construct a raised bed that is taller than twelve inches, (especially if it is longer than five feet). As mentioned before, after a few watering, the soil will compact slightly, becoming heavier and the pressure may well cause your beds to bulge out on the sides in mid-span. So for beds of this height you will require cross supports. Place them in the middle of the span, right across the width. This will prevent the two sides from bulging out. If you purchased your raised beds from a garden center these supports were probably included in the package but if your raised beds are home-made, you will have to make your own, using composite plastic, aluminum or wood.

Soil Depth for Most Vegetables

The Roots Need Adequate Depth

Most nutrients in garden beds are to be found in the top six inches of the soil. The reason is that most vegetable root growth happens in this shallow depth. The key nutrients like fertilizers and compost are added from the top and then tilled in lightly. Mulches also, are applied on the top surfaces of the beds from time to time; they eventually decompose to add extra nutrients to the soil, enriching it.

If moisture and nutrients are available deeper in the soil, tap roots will grow down to reach them. This brings additional trace minerals to the vegetable plants as well. The larger the plant, the deeper the roots will travel. Deeper roots anchor the plant much firmer into the bed, enabling it to withstand strong winds or heavy rains and saturated soil. Plants with big leaves and shallow root systems like broccoli, cauliflower and Brussels sprouts will need staking to make sure they do not fall over as they develop and reach maturity.

Do some research before you prepare the raised beds for your upcoming garden since the root depth of different vegetables can vary considerably. This will determine where you plant certain veggies and to what depth the soil needs to be prepared.

Raised beds which have been set on a gravel surface or a concrete patio will not allow roots to grow any deeper down than the depth of the beds. In this case, make sure you know the depth requirements for the different crops. You can compensate for an impenetrable ground surface by making the beds higher, providing enough root space. The average raised bed is between eight and twelve inches tall, but experienced gardeners have planted in beds with sides exceeding three feet. While these beds are ideal for crops with deep roots, you have to provide good drainage by drilling a number of holes towards the bottom of your beds, right along the sides.

The Height of Mature Vegetables

Tall Plants Blocking Sunlight

Plants are dependent on sunlight for their growth. Plan the layout of your raised garden beds so that they benefit as much as possible from sunlight throughout the day. You have to orientate them in such a way that they will enjoy the maximum amount of sun exposure. Your beds should therefore be arranged to all face in a southerly direction, placing them horizontally one after the next. As the sunlight moves from the east to the west, optimum exposure will be able across all the beds from side to side. Furthermore, this placing will prevent taller plants from blocking the sunlight that their adjacent neighbors need.

I am sure you have seen garden layouts running north-south, in other words, vertically. Some gardeners reason that this arrangement will minimize the possibility of one plant shading another. This may work effectively if you want to grow different varieties of vegetables in the same raised bed. The tallest plants should then be located at the northern side or rear end with the shorter ones in front of them.

No matter how you decide to arrange the raised beds in your garden, it is still important to establish the eventual height of your mature plants to make sure every single one of them will receive the sunlight it needs to flourish and grow to its full potential. In the front or south side, you can plant veggies like radishes and lettuce, following with medium size plants. The tallest vegetable plants will make up the rear or north side of your bed. Remember that those veggies that need trellises like peas and pole beans can easily block out most of the sunlight, so take care where you place them in your bed.

Wind may damage tall plants; their height makes them more vulnerable so they will have to be safely secured to trellises. You will be wise to place them next to a windbreak.

A strong, well-developed root system will provide your plant with the nutrients and moisture it needs to produce the best fruit. If you understand the basic factors about the root systems of your plants; their depth requirements and behavior, you will surely be able to provide them with the ideal conditions for maximum growth and bountiful harvests.

Chapter 3

Raised Bed Gardens: Soil Preparation

Every successful gardener will tell you that soil preparation comes first when you aim for a bountiful harvest. Without proper soil, you may as well throw in the towel before you even begin. Initially you should focus all your attention on the condition and quality of soil you are going to use. A good quality soil will ensure that your vegetable plants grow to their full potential and that you will not spend too much valuable time fighting pests and weeds.

Following are a few tips for mixing rich and fertile soil to suit all your planters and garden beds. Your locality may influence the type of soil you will need to a small degree, but these basic principles are applicable everywhere, regardless of where you live.

1. Topsoil does not Always Contain Organic Matter

Purchased soil often looks quite promising: dark in color, well screened and clean. This might not always be an indication of what it actually contains. It may well be a good growing medium though without any of the vital organic matter that is essential for growth. Therefore, you should always inquire from the attendant at the garden center what the soil consists of and what its origin is. You should assume that some extra feeding would be necessary to build up this soil to the standards needed for successful gardening.

2. Revitalize Soil Annually

Usually new gardens will do fairly well during their initial year even though no additional matter was added to amend the soil. The reason for this is that the available nutrients, organic matter and trace minerals have not been tapped yet. However, after one or two seasons of successive gardening, the crops will have used up all the riches in the soil. That is why it is so important that you revitalize your gardening soil regularly.

A wonderful solution is to plant 'green manure' as a cover crop after the first two seasons of growing vegetables. These crops are very easy and simple to grow and have many benefits. As soon as the cover crop has matured, chop it up and then dig it lightly into your soil. Now your soil has been replenished with fresh organic matter. Consider growing leguminous crops like alfalfa or fenugreek since they will fix the atmospheric nitrogen in such a way that it can be used as nutrients by the plants. This type of green manure has many benefits; their roots will loosen the soil, bringing the deeper nutrients nearer to the surface of your garden beds. While you chop up the manure and work it into the ground as well as the activity of the roots will aerate your soil, thus improving the drainage for future crops.

3.   Soil must be Crumbly, Fluffy and Light

You want to make it as easy as possible for the roots of your plants to be able to work their way through the layers of soil in search of moisture and nutrients. Compacted and dense soil will make this essential task of plant roots very difficult and they will spend so much energy struggling to get to the nutrients that not much will be left for the rest of the plant to grow. You can easily facilitate better root growth by lightening your garden soil. This is turn will lead to better vegetative growth and you will see the positive results when your plants start to flourish.

How do you know if your soil is light enough? A simple test is to push your finger into it. You should have no trouble to poke it in up to the third knuckle of the finger. If you struggle to achieve this then you will have to lighten the soil by adding peat moss and working it into the top layer. I have already mentioned that peat moss is acidic by nature, so you will most probably have to add lime. Always enquire about the pH level of the soil you purchase. You need to know if lime will be necessary. Acidic soil is commonly found in most areas of our country so lime is usually needed, although there are regions that have alkaline soil. Many gardeners prefer to use vermiculite for lightening the soil because it does not break down at the same speedy rate as the peat moss.

4.   The Ultimate Amendment for Soil: Compost

Making your own compost is easy and can save you extra expense. Many gardeners have a compost heap in their back gardens. Compost consists of organic material filled with nutrients to turn normal soil into a rich medium for all your plants. Use this valuable resource correctly and wisely and you can be sure of a prolific vegetable garden. Instead of adding compost to the soil right after harvesting, rather postpone it to two or three weeks before you plant your next crop. You want to prevent a sudden downpour from washing away all that wonderful richness in the compost and undo all your hard work.

The general idea amongst many people who consider a compost heap an unsightly, smelly mess is truly a misconception. If you go about it the correct way, your compost heap will be neat and tidy with a wonderful rich and earthy aroma. Veteran gardeners will tell you that active compost heaps should not be smelly. If your plot is too small to allow for a larger compost pile, you can purchase a sealed composter. This device contains smells and is small and tidy in appearance. Because they are sealed, they are immune to dogs, mice, raccoons and such-like critters.

A composter in your garden has an additional benefit; it will take care of all the dead plant matter left after the harvest. After your last tomatoes have been harvested, carefully remove all the 'skeletons' from the plants, break or chop it into smaller pieces and simply throw them into the compost pile. It is a wonderful way to re-use all plant residues in your garden to make a contribution to the nutrient-rich compost for your future crops. Just inspect the dead plant matter carefully for any diseases before you add it to the composter.

5.   Organic Fertilizers are the Best Choice

Do not be overly enticed by all the many product claims you read on the packaging of chemical fertilizers. They may be true, but the advantages often do not last and are rather short-lived. You will have to reapply them regularly after each planting. In the end, the benefits of these commercial fertilizers may be lessened to some extend because they do not improve the condition of the soil, the most important aspect of successful gardening.

I would therefore suggest that when you find yourself short of compost, to make use of an organic fertilizer. It will also give your little seedlings an instant boost. Canola meal is one of the popular fertilizers. This material is finely ground and lightweight, making it very easy to sprinkle onto your beds. On top of that, it is relatively inexpensive and free of weeds. (Some kinds of manures may include weeds). Make sure to mix the canola meal lightly into the topsoil because mice love it and may attack your beds. For the same reason, take care where you store your bag. It should be well sealed and in any dry spot where mice will not be able to reach.

6.   Rock Phosphate

If you a new gardener, using the plot or raised bed for the first time, you will probably be able to use the basic soil for one or two years. After this, you will have to add some source of phosphorus to it. Your crops will grow steadily and vigorously and mature early because of the addition of this element. You will have larger-sized vegetables and fruit in autumn. Crops, which mature earlier, will better avoid summer drought and be less vulnerable to disease and frost. Rock phosphate also contains a number of minor elements like zinc, boron, iodine and nickel, all necessary in smaller doses for plants to grow optimally. Furthermore, rock phosphate works long-term, thus releases its elements slowly so that the plant will benefit over a longer period.

Although phosphate is such an essential contributor to plant growth it is often overlooked even by more experienced gardeners. I strongly advise you to buy a bag and sprinkle a handful or two into your beds from time to time. A sack of phosphate will store well and last for years. Make a note to mix some rock phosphate into your raised vegetable beds at least every couple of years.

After reading this chapter, I am sure you understand the importance of paying attention to all the different aspects of your soil; its structure, the organic matter it contains, its drainage and the condition of the bottom or ground soil. If you focus on these elements all your expectations for a lush, high-yielding vegetable garden will be met. Your time will be spent on harvesting rather than on fighting diseases and pests and you will end up a happy, contented gardener.

Chapter 4

How to Construct Raised Bed Gardens

Many eager gardeners with rather poor quality soil in their plots have been given new life by a raised garden. Instead of fighting a losing battle with poor ground soil, raised beds are built above ground and places you in complete control of the quality and texture of the soil.

The Making of Raised Bed Gardens

Most popular are contained raised beds since they are wonderful for herb and vegetable gardens. They also work very well for planting flowers. Even fruits like grapes, strawberries, raspberries and blueberries are quite happy to grow in them.

Frames can be constructed from various materials but wood is the champion since it is inexpensive and very easy to use and work with. Other options are concrete blocks, brick or natural stone and although they are also good options, you have to consider the extra expense and the labor needed to construct them.

Probably the simplest and cheapest route to follow would be to make use of bales of straw or hay. Lay them out in any pattern or configuration you might desire, continue to fill them with compost and soil and start planting. The downside of using hay is that it will certainly not last you a lifetime; the straw or hay will slowly decompose, leaving you with about one to two years of use. On the other hand, this is a handy temporary solution if you need time to consider structures that are more permanent or want to try out different locations. It is also not such a big deal to replace the bales of hay from time to time.

I will focus on the different steps to construct your own wooden framed raised bed since that is the most common material used.

Select the Best Site

Most plants especially herbs, vegetables and some flowers need a minimum of eight hours sunlight every day. Once you have decided which plants you want to start with, select the site that will give your plants optimum exposure to the sun throughout the season. The area should be level and proximity to the water source will make a big difference to your chores. Remember that you will need room to move around your beds while tending them.

Decide on the Shape and Size of the Garden

When considering the size of your raised bed garden, bear in mind that all areas of it must be easily accessible to you without you having to step into any of the beds. Soil in raised beds has the advantage of staying loose and not compacted like conventional ground soil, so you do not want to have to crawl into your beds to reach all the plants. If you restrict the beds to four feet in width, you will be able to reach the center of the beds from both sides.

If the only space available is against a fence or wall, do not make your bed wider than three feet. It does not matter so much how long you decide to make your raised beds. The main problem comes when the width restricts easy access to all the plants.

As far as the depth is concerned, the average is around six inches because various vegetables will grow quite well in soil of this depth. However, bigger is often better, so if you are in a position to construct your bed allowing for soil twelve inches deep, so much the better. If you are lucky to have a good quality subsoil without rocks and not clay-like, dig it up, using your garden fork to loosen it and then your bed need not be too deep. Anything between six and eight inches will suffice since you now have the extra ground soil for those roots that want to dig deeper.

Without good ground soil to use for extra depth or in case you plan to cultivate crops like parsnips and carrots which require deeper soil, plan to make your raised bed ten inches or more deep.

Prepping your Site

The decisions about the shape and size of your beds have been taken, so now you can continue to prepare this site. The amount of prepping needed depends on how deep you are going to make your beds and which plants you want to grow in them.

For most vegetables you will only need six inches of soil depth to keep them happily growing. Start by placing layers of newspaper, cardboard or landscape fabric on top of the ground soil of the site you chose. Continue to pile the soil with its amendments on top. If you want to provide more room for those roots that like to grow deeper, first dig out all the existing sods. Now loosen the ground soil to a depth of around twelve inches with your garden fork or shovel. Then go ahead with your mixture of rich soil and compost.

Construction of the Bed

If you want your bed to last, use a rot-resistant type of wood like cedar. New composite lumbers are also available to construct the raised bed. I find that the 2 by 6 lumber works perfectly since it is very easy to handle and the six inches depth it provides is perfect. Start by cutting all the different pieces to the correct size.

Now you have to attach them to one another to form a frame. There are many different ways to attach the parts. An easy approach it to place a smaller piece of wood, in each corner and then attach both sides to this wooden block. Otherwise make butt joints in each corner, drill and then screw the corner panels together using galvanized screws.

Make Sure the Frames are Level

Although this sounds like a trivial detail, it is very important for your frames to be level all over. An uneven bed will cause water to run to one side of your garden and accumulate there while the opposite side will be left without the benefit of enough moisture. It is easy to rectify this situation; simply remove some soil at ground level from under the higher part of the frame. This should leave you with the desired effect.

Fill Up Your Garden

One of the main attractions of raised bed gardens is to give you the change to create the perfect soil mixture for your plants. Make good use of this opportunity and fill your beds up with rich, good quality topsoil, rotted manure and compost. Rake it level and you are ready to start planting your seeds or seedlings.

Maintenance

Raised beds filled with a good soil mixture will have very low maintenance. After the harvesting is done each season, I would suggest that you add some manure and compost to the top layer of soil before planting again. If your beds do not hold plants all year round, you can use the opportunity to mix in compost and manure several inches deep. To prevent weeds from growing and keep moisture in, add mulch to the top layer of your soil. The retention of moisture is quite important since these raised beds with their loose soil mixture drain quicker than the conventional garden beds.

Now that you have made your raised beds and filled them with the best quality soil mixture, we will proceed to talk about the best vegetables to grow in this garden.

Chapter 5

The Best Vegetables for Raised Beds

Growing vegetables and herbs in raised bed gardens has grown in popularity because it is so much easier than cultivating in a more conventional garden. This has inspired even those with so-called green thumbs to take up this worthy venture.

There are many reasons for the popularity of raised beds amongst gardeners. Firstly, you the gardener are in control of the quality of the soil you use. You can mix it to cater exactly to your specific needs instead of having to depend on the existing soil in your garden. Secondly, since the beds are raised, no one will step on it and the soil will not become compacted. This means that all the excess water will be able to drain away quickly. Lastly, you will have a longer season for growing your vegetables because soil in raised beds warms up much quicker when spring arrives.

You can grow almost anything in these raised beds, but some veggies are real stars in this regard and will flourish to their hearts' content in a raised bed garden.

1.   Root Vegetables

All root vegetables just love growing in raised bed. Beets, carrots, parsnips and radishes will prosper as the rock-free and loose soil allows them to spread their roots and make use of the available space. Plants that produce root vegetables need a specific type of soil and a raised bed gives you total control over which mixture you fill the beds with. The soil used for root vegetables must be clear of debris and rocks or clay if you want your veggies not to be misshapen. The roots must be able to grow freely without any hindrances.

2. All Leafy Greens

Lettuce, kale and spinach among other greens hate to get their feet wet for long. If their roots get soggy, they will not perform well. Soil in a raised bed is quick draining so your beautiful green lettuces will never have to sit with their roots in water. Another reason why these veggies are a wonderful choice for raised beds is that they enjoy cool weather. The soil in these beds warm up quicker than the surrounding ground, so you can start planting much earlier and get in more plentiful harvests before the summer with its heat descends. Remember that the more you harvest, the better these leafy greens will produce.

3.   Onions

You should seriously consider growing onions if you are starting with a raised bed garden for the first time. Onions are very at home in these surroundings for three reasons. The quick draining soil in a raised bed suits them perfectly. Secondly, they need enough time to grow to maturity and lastly they require lots of organic matter. It is easy to fulfil all these needs since you can control the quality of soil in your raised beds.

Therefore, always add lots of compost to the soil if you plan to plant onions. If you are growing your onions from seeds, you should know that they will need at least one hundred days before they reach maturity so in any area with four distinct seasons, your time is limited. Raised beds with its warmer soil will give you and your onions the time span they need. The soil also heats up earlier in the season and therefore your little seedlings will have a good head start.

4. Tomatoes

Most varieties of tomatoes are gluttonous feeders that will need plenty of nutrients in their soil to be able to thrive. Raised beds give you the opportunity to customize the soil to fit these greedy plants and help them to produce plump, healthy fruit. Stakes and tomato cages are a little more unstable in loose soil, so choose the varieties that will not grow too heavy or raise your bed a bit higher so that the plants can grow down over the sides instead of going upwards. This will also give your vegetable garden a wonderful lush look as well.

5.   Potatoes

Harvesting potatoes in conventional gardens can be a chore and real backbreaking work. That is one of the reasons for growing them in raised beds. They also like hilly soil all around their shoots while they grow and this you can contain and manage in a raised bed. Furthermore, they require loamy, loose and quick draining soil because they need to be able to spread out easily and freely as they grow. In loose soil, they are less likely to rot and it has been found that the tubers will be bigger in raised bed gardens. You can also expect a higher yield.

I have only mentioned a few of the vegetables that grow extra well in a raised bed. For a novice gardener these will be the easiest vegetables to start with, but do not feel you have to restrict your choices to these five kinds at all. With the right information and careful planning, there is nothing to keep you from embarking on growing vining veggies as well. Grow them on trellises, vertically for a great yield and wonderful display when they start to produce. So, do not allow anything to hold you back from trying out new vegetable plants. With the raised beds properly set up, you will turn into a great, enthusiastic, and experienced gardener in no time.

Chapter 6

High-Yielding Garden: The Secrets

You probably will not believe me if I tell you that it is quite possible to harvest almost a half tons of beautiful, tasty organic veggies from a fifteen by twenty foot garden plot. What if I tell you that you can get one hundred pounds of lush tomatoes from a four by twenty four foot plot or twenty pounds of crunchy carrots from only twenty-four square feet? Yes, these unbelievable yields can certainly be achieved and it is easier than you imagined. For your garden to be so super productive, all you have to do is work out the right strategies for your specific circumstances.

I will now provide you with seven strategies for high yielding vegetable gardening. These are all tried and tested methods from experienced super productive gardeners who know how to use the space in their gardens optimally.

1.   Build Up Rich Soil

The quality of your soil is by far the most important contributing factor to productivity. All the expert gardeners agree on this. Therefore, to start off, you need deep soil, rich in organic matter to encourage extensive, healthy root systems that are then able to get to all the water and nutrients. A strong root system in the soil will result in extra productive plant growth outside the soil.

What is the fastest and easiest manner to obtain such a deep fertile soil? Plant your vegetables in raised beds. Plants in rows on the ground will yield four times less than those planted in the same space in raised beds gardens. This is firstly due to the efficient use of space; no space is wasted on paths between rows. Secondly, the rich, loose soil in raised beds will increase the productivity of your plants and help them to grow to their full potential.

By the way, it has been proven that you will also save lots of time if you grow your veggies in raised beds. A researcher wrote down how many hours he spent planting and maintaining his thirty by thirty foot garden in raised beds. He was astounded to find that he only had to spend twenty-seven hours during a five-month season from May to October. On top of this, his harvest during these five months came to a thousand nine hundred pounds of all kinds of fresh veggies! He calculated that he produced enough crops for a family of three for an entire year.

You may well ask how this is possible. Well, the plants in raised bed gardens are planted close together with the result that they prevent weeds from growing and therefore you spend a lot less time fighting these unwelcome intruders. Your garden is also less spread out which makes fertilizing, harvesting and watering a lot more efficient.

2. Rounded Out Beds

The surface shape of the beds will also make some difference. For example, a bed with a width of five foot along its frame, if rounded on top into a gentle arch, will mean that you now have an extra surface of a foot across for planting your seedlings. Maybe it does not sound like so much, but when you multiply this number with the length of the bed, you will realize what a difference it will make to your total planting area.

The longer the bed, the more the increase in planting space will amount to if you round the top surface. Therefore, if your bed is twenty foot in length you can increase the area from a hundred to hundred and twenty square feet. A twenty percent gain can make a tremendous difference when you look at the total output you can obtain from this.

The crops that are best suited to this kind of beds are greens like lettuce and spinach; they can be planted all along the edges.

3.   How to Space Smartly

In order to obtain the highest yield possible from every bed, you have to arrange the plants in the best space-saving arrangement. Rows or square patterns do not work well in this regard. Using triangles to stagger your plants will enable you to fit in ten to fourteen more vegetable plants in a bed.

However, there are some plants that do not like to be crowded; they will not be able to grow to their optimum size if they are too close together. It is not always the number of plants per square foot that will yield the most. One research gardener found that his romaine lettuces actually produced more weight-wise when he planted them ten inches apart instead of eight inches like previously.

Plants that are too tightly spaced together may experience stress and they will end up being more prone to disease and susceptible to attacks by insects.

4.   Growing Upwards

Regardless of the size of your raised bed garden, you will always be able to grow more plants if you go vertical. Vining crops which love to seek more space, like pole beans, tomatoes, peas, melons and squash can be assisted by trellises, cages, stakes or fences to grow in an upward direction, rather than along the ground.

You will also save a lot of time by growing your veggies vertically. Maintenance and harvesting will be quicker because you are able to see clearly, where everything is. The air circulation amongst the foliage of vertical plants is increased, making them better prepared to withstand fungal diseases.

Consider planting your vining crops alongside one side of your raised bed. Erect two sturdy posts at the ends and then cover the space between them with string or nylon mesh. This will create a climbing area for your crops. To help them on their way, you can tie the vines to the mesh as soon as they have grown high enough. You will see that even the heavier fruits like melons and squash will be safe, as their stems grow thicker to support them. So do not worry yourself about securing these fruit.

5.   Mix Them Up

Mixing up compatible crops will also save space in your raised beds. The classic combination of the so-called three sisters is an old Native American favorite and includes beans, corn and squash. The strong cornstalks can easily support your pole beans, leaving more than enough space for the squash to grow along the ground. They will provide enough shade to prevent any competing weeds from growing in your beds. This is a wonderful compatible combination that has been successfully implemented for ages. There are many other combinations that work just as well. Try combining basil, tomatoes and onions; brassicas or peas and leaf lettuces; radishes, carrots and onions; and celery and beets.

6.   Successions Lead to Success

If you grow crops that are acclimatized to succeed each other throughout the season, you can grow a lot more in the same raised bed. In other words, plant will succeed each other after the harvest, allowing for a greater variety as well. I will give you an example: Follow a crop of lettuces early in the season with corn that matures rapidly, followed by overwintered garlic or more greens.

Keep the following three things in minds to make the most of succession plantings:

- Start with transplants instead of seeds. You will save about a month of growing time since seeds take that much longer and your plants will mature quicker.
- Choose those varieties that are fast growing.
- Before each planting, add about half an inch of compost to your topsoil, working it in, (it comes to around two cubic feet for every hundred square feet). This will replenish the soil and make sure that the next crops will get the nutrients they need.

7.   Stretch the Season

If you can find a way to add a week or two to the beginning or last part of the season, you will buy time to invest in extra crops. For instance, plant kale, turnips or leaf lettuce as early as possible and then add another harvest of tomatoes right at the end tail of your season.

When you start to plant earlier than usual when the weather is still cold, make sure you keep the air all around the plants warm. For this, you can use row covers, cold frames, cloches or mulches.

If you want to start your gardening season with vegetables that actually prefer warmer weather conditions, like peppers, melons and eggplants, there is a way. Provide them with an extra blanket of heating the soil as well as the air around them. Start to pre-heat the cold soil six to eight weeks prior to the last frost. Cover it with IRT, infrared-transmitting mulch or sheets of black plastic. Plastic will absorb the heat from the sun and warm up the soil underneath.

With either of these options in place, cover the whole bed with a tunnel made of clear plastic with slits in it to allow some of the heat to escape if necessary. As soon as the temperature of the soil reaches sixty five to seventy degrees Fahrenheit, you can set out your plants. Now cover the mulch or black plastic using straw to make sure it does not trap excessive heat. As soon as the danger of more frost is past, or the temperature has risen enough, get rid of the plastic tunnel. Re-install it at the end of summer when the cold set in again.

Chapter 7

Combinations for Companion Planting

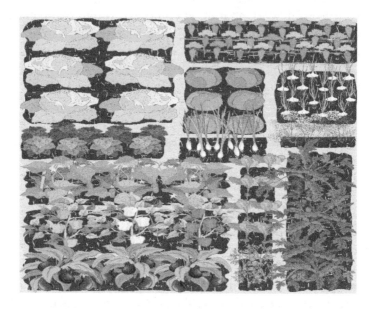

Different planting combinations can help in various ways; some will improve flavor, while others will ensure maximum yield of vegetables and fruit. Still other plant companions will aid in repelling parasites and pests or improve the health of the soil. Other benefits include the aid of pollination and regulation of shade.

I will now continue to advise you on the very best combinations you can implement to make full use of all these benefits and ensure your raised vegetable garden as productive and efficient as possible.

Vegetables

Tomatoes

Tomatoes and potatoes belong to the same plant family. Their combination is best avoided – do not plant them together. Tomatoes, however, will truly benefit from the presence of onions, basil, sage, rosemary and parsley.

Potatoes

This staple veggie will be very happy to grow alongside any variety of the cabbage family, peas or beans. Although they love squash, they do not want pumpkins or cucumbers as companions. Potato beetles and nematode worms are just two of the enemies potatoes have to defend themselves against. You can scare them off by growing marigold and basil close to your potatoes, as the former will repel these pests. Other pests can be avoided by planting alyssum as ground cover. This cover attracts some insects that in turn feed on the pests.

Peppers

Lettuce, radishes and spinach love to grow in the shade created by taller pepper plants. They will repay their umbrella plant by suppressing the weeds. Chives and basil actually improve the peppers' flavor while repelling some bothering pepper pests. Another good idea is to plant leeks, onions and garlic. Peppers with their variety of bright colors will add luster to any garden so plant them in combination with petunias, marigolds and geraniums for a lovely display in your ornamental garden. These flowers will ensure your peppers grow free of pests.

Eggplants

These exotic purple vegetables are popular amongst many home gardeners, and unfortunately with numerous damaging pests as well. Tarragon and thyme will help to fight off some of the insect pests. Spinach growing in the eggplants' shade, will not only flourish but also prevent weeds from growing. Eggplants require enough nitrogen for their roots and therefore you can plant beans to assist with this. Choose the shorter varieties that will not block sunlight, though.

Carrots

Radishes and lettuce make good bedfellows for carrot plants. So do leeks and onions because they ward off carrot flies. Just remember that onions can be planted in proximity to carrots but not in the exact same bed, otherwise they will compete for the same resources. Carrots are quite happy with leeks close by in the same bed. Marigold and chives will also repel insects and be a benefit to carrots but separate carrots from parsnips and dill.

Broccoli

There are quite a number of plants that make excellent companions for your broccoli, like dill, garlic, onions, sage, basil and celery. These are all aromatic plants that will attract some of the enemies of the pests that like to attack broccoli. They also ward off some of the predators of broccoli. Celery and onions will improve your broccoli's flavor and plant nasturtiums and beets in the same bed to provide the relatively high need for calcium this vegetable has. Other plants which you can happily combine with broccoli are cucumbers, bush beans, potatoes, radishes and lettuce.

Cabbage

Dill makes a wonderful companion for cabbage and other cruciferous veggies. The reason for this is that dill attracts the wasps that prey on numerous cabbage pests. Onions and celery will both benefit your cabbage plants while chamomile will enhance its flavor.

You may grow potatoes in the same bed as your cabbage but refrain from using other members belonging to this nightshade family. The latter include tomatoes, eggplants and peppers.

Cauliflower

Cauliflowers and beans are best friends, so plant them together. Celery, onions and dill act as protectors for cauliflower and zinnias all around this veggie will provide added protection. Ladybugs like zinnias blooms and will prey on cauliflower pests. On the other hand, it is not a good idea to plant strawberries in the vicinity of cauliflowers as the slugs they attract them will damage your cauliflower heads.

Cucumbers

While nasturtiums will repel all cucumber beetles, beans, carrots, peas, radishes and beets will also grow nicely with cucumbers. Sunflowers and marigolds will provide the same protection that nasturtiums do.

Squash

This vegetable likes the same bedfellows as cucumbers. Encircle your squash with beets, radishes and carrots. Squashes need more nitrogen that can be made available by legumes planted in the very same rounded bed. Complete this advantageous setting with a few marigolds and nasturtiums.

Corn

Corn is not very picky and can be planted together with about any member belonging to the squash and legume family in order to make up the popular three sisters combination. You can even include peas and beans, melons and cucumbers. Lettuce and potatoes also grow well with corn in the same raised beds.

Asparagus

Veggies to avoid near your asparagus are potatoes, garlic and onions, but the combination with tomatoes and carrots will work well. Ward off asparagus beetles from the young tender roots by planting marigolds, chrysanthemums, or herbs like dill, basil, and parsley nearby. You may also consider tomatoes because these contain solanine, a toxin against these beetles.

Spinach

This vegetable does not like too much direct sun so the shade provided by taller plants such as eggplant, beans, cauliflower, cabbage, celery and radishes will be welcomed. Onion and squash are also good companions.

Strawberries

Cruciferous veggies like cabbage should be avoided near your strawberry beds but feel free to plant lettuce, beans and spinach in their vicinity. Plant thyme to form a border around your strawberry patch; it will help keep worms at bay.

Raspberries

Damage from fungal diseases or harmful insects can be prevented by planting marigold and garlic in combination with your raspberries. Harlequin beetles will stay away if you grow turnips in the same bed. However, do not consider potatoes, blackberries or tomatoes near them because these plants may transmit viral diseases.

Roses

Traditionally garlic plants have always played a companion with roses since this pungent herb will repel most insects. That said, you might decide to rather make use of garlic, marigolds and chives in a non-ornamental garden.

Herbs and Flowers in Your Vegetable Garden

As you have seen, quite a number of flowering plants are beneficial to your veggie garden and may help in various ways. Make liberal use of them, as their blooms will attract the insects your veggie plants need for pollination and to keep pests at bay. They will also add an aesthetic dimension to your vegetable patch and make it look colorful and lush.

Numerous culinary herbs do double duty in your vegetable garden. Not only are they real bee magnets, they also confuse unwanted insects with their intense, pungent smells and direct them away from your precious vegetable plants.

Here are a few herbs and ornamentals to assist you in your garden and which can be planted in combination with your vegetables.

Marigold

Calendula, or pot marigolds, Mexican and French marigolds are just great in any ornamental or vegetable garden. Planted in patches throughout your garden and they will control the nematodes and help to repel insect pests like whiteflies. Just remember to keep them away from your cabbage and beans.

Sweet Alyssum

This plant grows low on the ground to spread out and cover the soil in a thick mat. This will prevent any weeds from growing and on top of that, they have fragrant flowers, which will attract many bees to pollinate your vegetable plants.

Sunflowers

Sunflowers with their beautiful large flowers will be an attraction in any garden. They offer wonderful cool shade for more tender plants and their strong stems act as support for plants with weaker stems. The yellow flowers attract lots of pollinators and they repel nematodes as well.

Chrysanthemums

Some of the substances contained in these plants are quite toxic to numerous insects, especially root nematodes and Japanese beetles.

Dahlias

Not only do dahlias have beautiful flowers, they continue to produce these striking flowers year after year, growing from their tubers underground. The additional benefit is that they repel nematodes.

Geraniums

Another very attractive plant that produces pretty flowers, this plant is quite effective in repelling beet leafhoppers, cabbageworms and Japanese beetles. Not just a pretty face!

Chives

You have already heard this small plant mentioned several times earlier and not without reason. With its pretty little flowers and thin leaves looking like grass, it will look good in any kind of garden and help to keep away all types of harmful pests like aphids. Plant them close to tomatoes, carrots and cruciferous vegetables, but stay away from peas and beans.

Dill

This herb is cherished not only for the subtle taste it lends to many dishes, but organic gardeners often utilize it to prevent pests from populating their cabbage and squash gardens. The large flowers are an attraction for predatory wasps as well as other insects that keep these pests from infiltrating. Dill attracts tomato hornworm, though, so be sure not to plant it anywhere near your peppers, potatoes or tomatoes.

Garlic

The Allium family includes onions, chives and leeks, but garlic is its most pungent member. They all do excellent work in repelling harmful insects and keeping them at bay. The sweet nectar in their flowers will attract bees as well as other pollinators.

Sage

Never plant cabbages or carrots without their protecting companion, sage. This herb is the archenemy of cabbage moths and carrot flies. It will benefit tomatoes too.

Basil

Who does not love the wonderful fragrance of a crushed basil leaf? Well, this is exactly why they repel mosquitoes, flies, and other harmful insects. They also add flavor to tomatoes and peppers.

Rosemary

There are no negative aspects to this plant at all; to the contrary, stunning rosemary is not only a must in every herb garden, it keeps almost all kinds of invasive insects at bay and its wonderful smell and flowers attract bees and pollinators.

Research is Important

Start your companion raised garden by deciding on which vegetables you want to grow. Then continue to do proper research to determine the plants that will flourish in your climate zone. Next, plan the layout of your garden. Before you start planting, determine which companion plants will benefit your selected vegetable plants. Lastly, make sure to utilize your available space to its maximum.

Companion gardening work wonderfully in the small spaces of raised beds or planters. Using this technique as well as thorough planning before you begin the raise bed vegetable garden will almost guarantee you continual supply of nutritious vegetables year round.

Chapter 8

How to Start a Raised Bed Vegetable Garden: FAQs

Nothing worth its while in life comes free, so we all accept that there will be a little effort involved in setting up the raised beds for our own vegetable garden. However, once that is done and taken care of, you will reap the benefits repeatedly throughout the seasons.

Garden boxes, as it is also called, consist of a frame made from a choice of various materials, which is then placed straight onto the ground in the area you have selected. It is then filled up with soil mixed with a choice of organic matter. Because it is raised above the ground, the frames will keep your garden weed-free and deter many pests. The frames also prevent soil erosion and soil compaction. It offers excellent drainage and saves space.

The experience of gardeners is that raised beds are super productive and extremely convenient. I will now address some of the frequently asked questions about how to go about when you start your own vegetable plants in garden boxes.

1.   Why consider raised beds for my vegetable garden?

If you are a very busy person with little free time, this is for you. It takes a lot less time managing raised beds than it would a complete garden plot and it is in fact a lot easier. If your gardening space is limited, the soil in your garden is of a poor quality or even if there is an area in your existing garden that is a real eyesore, raised beds can solve all your problems. Many gardeners find that raised beds give their vegetable gardens a neater and tidier look and that these beds produce quite a bit more veggies.

2.   When is a good time to set up the raised beds?

You can start anytime you want so do not postpone it too long. They have to be ready when the growing season starts so I would suggest setting it up in the early spring.

3.   How big should my raised beds be?

You determine the size of your beds as long as they fit the available space, of course. The general rule is not to make them wider than four feet along one side. You will find that this width allows you easy access from all sides for your weeding, cultivating, and harvesting. Anything wider and you might find yourself stretching to reach all the different areas of your beds.

How high you decide to make your beds is also your choice. Disabled or elderly gardeners should carefully consider which height would be convenient for them; usually it should be the height of your waist. This makes it easy to sit in the sides while you do your maintenance and prevent you from having to bend down too much.

4.   If I am not a handy person how can I make a raised bed?

You do not have to construct your own beds from scratch. Many
garden centers sell ready-made ones or frames that are very simple to
assemble yourself. Just follow the instructions, they will show you how
to do it one-step at a time. The fact is that these beds can be
constructed from a number of different materials, like metal, wood,
plastic or even cinder blocks.

5.   Is it necessary to prepare the soil under my raised bed?

Although it is not a hard and fast rule, I would strongly recommend
that you do it. If you loosen this soil and get rid of all the debris and
rocks, the roots of your plants can reach down deeper into the soil for
the nutrients and water they need. This will mean a stronger and
healthier root system that in turn will ensure plants that are more
productive.

This may sound like a lot of extra work, but you need to do it only
once – right in the beginning before you assemble your bed. Dig down
to around twenty-four inches of the surface, adding humus, topsoil,
compost and some extra organic matter. The soil underneath your bed
should be similar to the soil in your raised bed.

6.   How many vegetable plants can I grow in my raised bed?

It depends on the type of plants you want to grow. In a four by four
bed, you will be able to accommodate up to six low growing vegetable
plants, for instance squash, cucumbers, zucchini and herbs. Plant a few
of the taller vegetables in the very center of your bed; tomatoes would
work well. If you have a longer bed, say around eight feet, you can set
up one or two trellises for your vining crops. Beans or peas will do
well.

7.   Which should I plant – seedlings or seeds?

The rules are the exact same as you would follow when you plan your vegetables in plots in the garden. Some crops will do better if you start with seedlings. These include perennial herbs, peppers and tomatoes. Others will be more successful if you sow the seeds straight into the raised beds. These include lettuces, beans, radishes, cucumbers, squash and basil.

8.   What is the best way to water my vegetables in raised beds?

You can always do it manually but take care when you water young tender seedlings that you do not damage them or wash away the soil around them. A drip irrigation system would be ideal since it regulates the amount of water your plants receive while providing the moisture in the correct doses.

Conclusion

Starting a raised bed garden is a great way to accommodate that budding little gardener in your family. It is the ideal way for kids to learn about nature; they will see the wonder of a little seedling emerging from the ground, growing tiny leaves and later develop into a mature plant with fruit. Planting in raised beds will make it convenient for both you and the young ones to reach every plant in the box without ending up with muddy feet or knees full of dirt.

Now that you have all the information needed, it is time to get going. Walk around your available space during the day to find a sunny location. Once you have decided where you want to place your raised bed, decide on the size and dimensions. The next step is to make a list of everything you will need, from the soil, compost and other materials, to the frames. Once your bed is up and filled up with the soil mixture, it is time to turn your attention to the plants. Select the type of veggies you want to grow according to the guidelines I have provided. If you want to grow plants from seeds, you will have to do some prior planning since it will take time for them to develop into seedlings ready to be planted outside in your box. Otherwise, you can purchase seedlings to plant directly into your raised beds.

Now most of the work is done and the fun part starts. While you wait for your veggies to grow, a little attention is needed; water them regularly and keep your eyes peeled for any pests or weeds. Then wait for the fruit to mature and start harvesting!

Growing vegetables in raised beds makes gardening a pleasure. With limited time and space, you can grow an abundance of food in a small area. The benefits are numerous; fewer weeds and pests, better drainage, better soil, no compacting of the soil, less pain potential for you, the gardener, to name but a few. Your friends will envy your neat, attractive garden and harvest of healthy, tasty vegetables.

Other Related Books

ISBN-13: 978-1545415115

ISBN-13: 978-1517773762

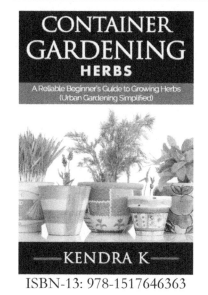

ISBN-13: 978-1517646363

ISBN-13: 978-1545073933

99990569R00036